MW01202144

Women Mystics in the Christian Tradition

Women Mystics in the Christian Tradition

Elizabeth A. Perry

Elizabeth A. Perry
2021

First Printing: 2021

ISBN 978-1-716-23840-6

Elizabeth A. Perry
Post Office Box 3487
Astoria, New York 11106

www.revbethperry.wordpress.com

Dedication

To Pixie,
who helped me locate the mystics,
and myself in the process.

Contents

Acknowledgements

Thank you to www.BeADisciple.com for their generous hosting of the workshop that accompanies this book. And for the support of Lisa Buffum and her www.BeADisciple.com staff over the past decade!

Thank you, as well, to all those who have shared in my women mystic workshops and courses in so many different incarnations over the past 30 years. You've all contributed to what I know and what I teach.

And finally, thank you to all of you who are or will teach this material yourself, to new generations of learners.

E. A. Perry

Introduction

I remember when I first read any writing from women mystics… It was in the mid-90's, in a bookstore, where I had just opened a book called *Women in Praise of the Sacred: 43 Centuries of Spiritual Poetry by Women,* edited by Jane Hirshfield.

And there on the pages were Rabi'a, Catherine of Sienna, and Mirabai! Marguerite Porete (who could resist that name!), Sappho, and Emily Dickinson! Teresa of Avila, Hildegard of Bingen, and Kadya Molodowsky! Bibi Hayati, Owl Woman, and the Queen of Sheba!

After that, there were many other books and many other websites and many other readings and songs and prayers and explorations! I took what I learned and shared it with others – speaking in bookstores, at women's conferences, to local congregations, etc.

Eventually, through BeADisciple.com, I focused a course on Christian women mystics, which numerous men and women have participated in, sharing their knowledge and experiences to broaden and deepen mine.

But throughout all of that, there was a single question running through my mind and through those courses:

Do these mystical women have anything of value to say to us today?

Do their situations, their experiences, their writings – in whole or in part – tell us something that we can apply to our faith today? Can they shed light on our desire for God, our desire for faithfulness, our desire for unity, our desire for understanding? Can they tell us anything that makes sense of the spiritual dance we have been in throughout our lives – or the dancing yet to come?

Overall, I believe that these ancient women, these prior women, have something to tell us all. They, and all the more recent mystics who I have learned about over the years, can bring us their wisdom to translate into our time… with some reservations that you'll read about later.

In this little book, you'll find the various documents that once floated around in my workshops and courses. There is space in each chapter for you to note any reflections or connections that you find with these women.

I hope you find it valuable and come back to it again and again!

Blessings,
Beth

Primer

Someone suggested I provide a primer for mysticism… but that is an impossible task, I think. In fact, I'd go so far as to say that anyone who tells you they can compact every view on mysticism into one short article, chapter, or book should probably be avoided.

But there are a few ways to give you a glimpse into mysticism before we enter our narrow and specific study.

First, let's look at some definitions…

Google Dictionary is a good example of the problem with a definition. It has two of them.

The first definition is:
> …belief that union with or absorption into the Deity or the absolute, or the spiritual apprehension of knowledge inaccessible to the intellect, may be attained through contemplation and self-surrender.

And the second definition is
> belief characterized by self-delusion or dreamy confusion of thought, especially when based on the assumption of occult qualities or mysterious agencies.

There's quite a difference between union with the divine and self-delusion, isn't there?

But that conflicted identity isn't just a problem for the new and superficial sources on the internet. My almost-ancient Concise Dictionary of Religion says this:
> The implications of this word are often unclear. In the study of religion it refers to the immediate experience of a divine-human relationship, and in particular to the experiences of oneness with a divine or transdivine BEING or STATE. It is difficult to study and describe because MYSTICS tend to claim that their

experience is self-authenticating, and that it cannot be satisfactorily expressed in words (Hexam, 1993).

Again, mystics could be those in a divine-human relationship, but they could also be those whose claims might be lies.

_____

_____

_____

Modern textbooks aren't much more help…

One on my shelf says this:
The intuitive perception of spiritual truths beyond the limits of reason (Fisher, Rinehart, 2016).

While another doesn't even include the word "mysticism" in the glossary but does say that "those known as mystics" … "claimed extraordinary experiences" which "invited close scrutiny," at least in Christianity (Corrigan, et al, 2011).

_____

_____

_____

So, if definitions fail to give us a primer for mysticism, perhaps taking a look at creeds might help….

Creeds reflect religious beliefs and faith; and faith is foundational to mystics so it might make sense to try that next.

There are mystics in all three of the Western Religions – Judaism, Christianity, and Islam. Judaism and Islam have mystic branches of the faith – Hassidism and Sufism. Christianity has mystics in all three branches of the faith: Catholicism, Orthodoxy, and Protestantism.

But the creeds of those three religions are very different, aren't they? While they share a common ancestor, common history, and common monotheistic theology, there is little other credal overlap.

Beyond the Western religions, there are also mystics in Eastern Religions: Hinduism and Buddhism – particularly Tibetan Buddhism, for example. And Daoism is considered by some scholars to be a completely mystical religion!

So, there are no creeds that overlap in all these religions, not even a basic theism, or belief in a divine being.

However, all religions have some version of the Golden Rule. *The Mysticism of the Golden Rule* by Nicholas Ayo, *The Mystic Power of the Golden Rule* by V. Fred Rayser, or other similar books might lend some foundation to a credal understanding of mysticism.

But I think it is more likely that Jeffrey Wattles' 1987 research paper on *Levels of Meaning in the Golden Rule* would likely show that the understandings of that rule are more different than similar.

_____

_____

_____

So, if definitions and religious creeds fail to give us a primer for mysticism, perhaps looking at the traits of mystics will help....

As you read in the definitions, there is an orientation toward experience, which does apply to mystics in multiple religions. Dancing Shakers in Christianity, Whirling Dervishes in Islam, and Jewish dancing with the Torah on Simchat Torah – all give examples of the use of physical experience to provide entry points for spiritual engagement.

We can accept that experience is a part of what it means to be a mystic.

But to say that all mysticism is solely experiential – that it is all beyond reason - is to ignore the wealth of learning birthed by mystics in various religions.

To say that mysticism is anti-intellectual or confused or delusional, denies the massive volume of poetry, song, theology, biography, and ritual that was brought to life by mystics, and developed in their mystical experiences.

_____

_____

_____

So static definitions, credal assertions, and reductionary categories could all limit mysticism in a way that isn't helpful to us.

Perhaps we should just move into the limited, narrow definition of mysticism that we'll deal with in this book, recognizing that it is one small slice of a larger pie than could possibly be contained in any book!

Chapter One: Our Definition of Mysticism

Our Definition of Mysticism

Aware of the dangers of misspeaking when talking about mystic experiences, Marguerite Porete wrote in the 13th century:

> *"Among you actives and contemplatives and you who are perhaps annihilated by true love, who will hear some of the powers of the pure love, the noble love, the high love of the Free Soul, and how the Holy Spirit put His sail in the Soul, as if in His ship, I beg of you out of love, says Love, to list carefully with the subtle understanding within you and with great diligence, for otherwise all those if they be not so who will hear this will understand badly"* (Wilson, 1984).

As I described in the Primer, defining mysticism could fill a book in itself! It is as elusive, personal, and nuanced as the experience of mysticism – and it's unlikely that all of us have the same definition in our heads when we begin this conversation.

However, we have one chapter for this overview and so we are going to use a very specific – and traditional – definition. *Mysticism is a personal experience of the Divine Reality, leading to unity or oneness with the Divine.*

Let's look at the three elements of that definition in a little more detail: personal experience, Divine Reality, and oneness with the Divine.

"Personal experience" tells us that mysticism is generally experienced individually rather than communally.

There can be times when a group of people have a mystical experience of God, but more often there might be a group living arrangement (convent, etc.) or ritual (dance, etc.) that lends itself to individuals having a mystic experience. In general, for the women we will look at, mystic experience is an individual experience.

It is an experience that could gather people together – mystics joining in community to support each other – but it also can isolate individuals from their community.

_____

_____

_____

"Divine Reality" tells us that the human individual is only half of the mystical experience! The other half is the Divine Reality.

The Divine Reality might be different in different religions – remember, mysticism is a part of all religions – but for Judaism, Christianity, and Islam, the Divine Reality is God.

For Christians, that Divine Reality also can include Jesus and the Holy Spirit. Christian mystic experiences can focus on any portion of the Trinity or on all three.

It's also important to note that while mystics seek an experience of God, it is God who initiates and fulfills the seeking.

Hadewijch, 13th century, wrote:

> *"To be one with love is an awesome calling and those who long for it should spare no effort. Beyond all reason they will give their all and go through all. For love dwells so deep in the womb of the Father that her power will unfold only to those who serve her with utter devotion"* (Wilson, 1984).

_____

_____

_____

"Oneness" tells us both an element of mysticism and the goal of it.

A mystical experience may include a sense of oneness with God – brief or lengthy - but the goal of mystical experiences is, ultimately, perpetual unity or oneness with God.

It's important to mention here, again, that specific religious beliefs are not significant to a discussion of mysticism and unity with God.

When you look at mystics across religions, or in the variations within a religion, you'll see that they have similar experiences, ways of understanding those experiences, and ways of talking about those experiences. So, it isn't important whether these mystical women are Catholic, Protestant, or Orthodox.

What is significant are the commonalities among mystics, particularly women mystics. And, again, I am narrowing the topic greatly for our discussion! The area of commonality for our discussion is love.

_____

_____

_____

Love is the experience these women have, it is the lens they use to understand that experience, and it is the language they use to describe the experience.

Union with the Divine, oneness with God, opens another world – a world of visions, miracles, suffering, knowledge – but that other world is understood and expressed in terms of the deepest of this-world relationships: love.

Catherine of Genoa wrote, in the 15th century:

   "And when I saw that Love accepted my cares and went about

its work, I turned toward the said Love, occupied with His gracious operations, and He with such love, solicitude, and justice did nothing more or less than was needed, satisfying me inwardly and outwardly. With this I was so contented that had he thrown me soul and body into hell, it would have seemed to me all love and good will..." (Wilson, 1987).

In particular, these mystical experiences are frequently expressed in the terms of romantic and sexual love. This is again an aspect of mysticism that crosses religious lines. It seems that of all the human relationships we have, romantic love comes the closest to enabling human beings to recognize and understand – and then communicate – about their mystical experiences.

Hdewijch, in the 13ᵗʰ century, wrote:

*"My yoke is sweet, my burden light," love's lover speaks with words conceived in love. ... What is this burden light in love, this yoke so sweet? It is that noble thrust inside, that touch of love in the beloved which makes him one with her, one will, one being, one beyond revoke. And there deeper digs desire and all that is dug up is drunk by love, for love's demands on love surpass the mind of man" (*Wilson, 1987).

For contemporary Christians, in contemporary church settings that frequently separate spirit and body, that may be a little unnerving! But recognize that mysticism is exactly about rejecting any separations – especially anything that might separate us from God – including the barriers between us and within us.

So, we have this very limited definition of mysticism: **a personal experience of unity or oneness with God, expressed in the language of love.**

In the next few chapters, we'll explore that definition through our ancient history, the traditional women mystics, and contemporary women mystics.

For reflection...

As you read the definition of mysticism and the quotes from various Christian women mystics, was there anything that particularly caught your attention?

_____
_____
_____

Did anything feel especially familiar or unusual?

_____
_____
_____

Was there anything that moved you - or made you uncomfortable?

_____
_____
_____

How will you displace that so you can move forward?

_____
_____
_____

Chapter Two: Scripture and Mysticism

Scripture & Mysticism

One ancient understanding of scripture was that it could be read on four levels.

The first, most superficial level, was the **literal** level – the level on which many people read scripture today.

The second, deeper, level was **metaphorical**: what was written represented something else.

The third, still deeper level was **spiritual**: what was written encouraged spiritual growth.

And the fourth, deepest, level was **mystical** – the level at which scripture moved humanity toward union with God. This is the level we hear very little about in typical sermons or Bible studies!

Below is a list of scriptures that lend themselves easily to mystical readings – especially the type we are talking about with its focus on love, intimacy, and ecstasy. As you read, consider whether you have ever read them this way – and if they remind you of any other scriptures not on this list.

The most obvious source of mysticism in scripture is the Song of Songs with its ecstatic love poetry, representing (among other things) the unity of God and humanity.

The Shunamite says:

> *"My love lifts up his voice, he says to me, 'Come then, my beloved... the season of glad songs has come...'"* Song of Songs 2:8, NRSV

> *"On my bed at night I sought... but could not find him... I caught him, would not let him go..."* Song of Songs 3:1-4, NRSV

_____

_____

_____

The language in the gospel of John also reflects mysticism in its focus on the unity of God, Jesus, and humanity.

> *"On that day you will know that I am in my Father, and you in me, and I in you."* John 14:20, NRSV

> *"Abide in me as I abide in you... I am the vine, you are the branches... I have said these things to you so that my joy may be in you, and that your joy may be complete."* John 15:4-11, NRSV

_____

_____

_____

But the love language of the prophets also lends itself to mystic interpretation...

> *"You have seduced me, Yahweh, and I have let myself be seduced..."* Jeremiah 20:7, NRSV

> *"I shall betroth you to myself forever... in faithful love and tenderness..."* Hosea 2:21-22, NRSV

_____

_____

_____

... as does the language of love and unity in the epistles, where unity with God is lived out in unity with each other.

"Beloved, let us love one another, because love is from God; everyone who loves is born of God and knows God. Whoever does not love does not know God for God is love... God is love and those who abide in love abide in God and God abides in them..." 1st John 4:7-16, NRSV

"We, although there are many of us, are one single body, for we all share in the one loaf." I Corinthians 10:16-17, NRSV

"...be of a single mind, one in love, one in heart and one in mind." Philippians 2:11, NRSV

_____

_____

_____

And, of course, there is the story of the union of Mary and the Holy Spirit in the incarnation, resulting in Mary's pregnancy and ecstatic song of love.

"The Holy Spirit will come upon you and the power of the Most High will overshadow you... 'My soul magnifies the Lord and my spirit rejoices in God my Savior...'" Luke 1:35, NRSV

_____

_____

_____

For reflection…

Were these familiar scriptures to you and did you already connect them to mysticism?

_____
_____
_____

Did the readings from yesterday have any impact on the way you heard the scriptures?

_____
_____
_____

If looking for the mystical level in all scripture is the deepest form of biblical interpretation, what other scriptures might also speak to our topic?

_____
_____
_____

Chapter Three: Jewish Women Mystics

Jewish Women Mystics

Judaism and mysticism existed before Christianity. However, the evidence of women in Jewish mysticism is slim, for several reasons.

First, in ancient Judaism, many women didn't write. Some weren't educated; others were oral people who taught and memorized but didn't write.

Second, later mystical Judaism (Hassidism) limited access to the Kabala (the mystical writings) to married men over 40 who were already well-versed in the Hebrew scriptures.

But we do find references to some Jewish women mystics, such as the **"Therapeutae."**

These were 1ˢᵗ century CE monastics in Alexandria, Egypt. They practiced austerity and meditation to perform physical and spiritual healings. They also held a weekly feast where they would drink "of the strong wine of God's love," then pray, sing, and dance throughout the night (Swidler, 1976).

In addition, these women were theologians, interpreting the law allegorically and writing hymns. "…their philosophical analysis of the Scriptures placed the Therapeutrides in a rarefied group of highly educated people in the ancient world" (Cohick, 2009).

_____

_____

_____

Oudil (or Udel) is a later example of Jewish mysticism. The 18ᵗʰ century daughter of the Baal Shem Tov, the recognized founder of Hassidic Judaism, was always with her father, studying and experiencing what he did.

One author said that people called her "Rebbe" (or teacher) and said that the "Shekinah rested on her face" (Sharma, 1987).

The **Shekinah** refers to the Kabala's teachings about the emanations of God – the energies that flow from various portions of the equivalent of God's body.

The Shekinah, a female emanation, flows from the feet of God and is most knowable emanation. The term Shekinah also applies to the people of Israel. It is the part of God so close to us that it can be part of us, and we can be part of it.

_____

_____

_____

In *Hassidic Tales of the Holocaust*, stories tell about 20th century women who certainly shared the mystical qualities of the Hassidim. One story tells of a woman named Sheila. Asked how she survived Bergen Belsen (a German concentration camp), she replied that it was a prayer she and others prayed "every minute of our wretched existence."

She described how in the days before the concentration camp was liberated, she fell ill with typhoid fever.
> *"Delirious and near death, I kept repeating the prayer... but its words were moving further away from me till I heard only the faint echo like the fluttering of wings in the distance. Suddenly, in the vacuum left by the prayer, I distinctly heard my mother's voice... "* (Eliach, 2011).

She had a vision of walking toward her mother's voice with a women's work detachment, all shaven-headed, hungry, and frozen.

Finally, she turned a corner, and

*"...at the doorway, she was standing – awaiting us with out-
stretched arms. She was dressed in her Sabbath finery, with a
snow-white apron. I fell into her waiting arms... My mother
hugged me, caressed me, and her gentle touch made my hair
grow... "* (Eliach, 2011).

In the vision, her mother gave her healthy food and, when the woman
awoke, the typhoid had left her.

Another story tells of a woman similarly dying of typhoid who
crawled to the top of a mound of dirt. She had a vision of her father
caressing her and telling her that liberation was on its way and she
would survive.

She was found a few days later, moved to a hospital, and did survive.
She later found out that the mound was a mass grave, and among
those buried in it was her own father.

_____

_____

_____

While these stories are not models for, nor duplicates of, the writings
of Christian women mystics, they do have some commonalities: the
emphasis on love and physical closeness, for example.

They let us know that Christian women mystics did not arise in a vac-
uum but were carrying on an ancient tradition that has continued into
our time.

For reflection...

How does this information about Jewish mystics connect to what you had already known or read?

_____
_____
_____

Do you see a connection between these Jewish origins and the quotes you read yesterday?

_____
_____
_____

Why might there be more similarities between women mystics in the two religions than between theologians in the two religions?

_____
_____
_____

Chapter Four: Medieval Christian Women Mystics

Medieval Christian Women Mystics

There are so many Christian women mystics that it is impossible to do justice to them all! I'm going to mention a few and share some excerpts from their writings but you'll find a bibliography at the back of this book.

First, let's look at women in the early church. In *Perpetua's Passion*, author Joyce E. Salisbury writes that the Roman world of the 1st and 2nd centuries was one in which people were longing for the presence of God (Salisbury, 1997).

The mystery religions flourished (like worship of the goddess Isis) as did magic and astrology – all designed to bring heaven a little closer to earth.

When Romans considered converting to Christianity, one of their primary questions would have been whether or not God was present in Christian gatherings. Christians were able to answer that question with references to trances, prophecy, and speaking in tongues, all evidence of an "ecstatic" state brought on by the presence of God.

So, there were women who lived in that first century or two, experiencing that richness of Christian worship.

_____
_____
_____

Then there were women who lived in the second or third century and grew up hearing about that earlier time.

These women often faced great persecution for their faith. Stories like *The Acts of Paul & Thecla* tell of these women, their mystical experiences, and the challenge they brought to the male hierarchy of the Roman church as well as to Roman society.
While these stories were not canonized, they hold valuable information for later generations, giving glimpses to the leadership

conflicts within the early church and with outside civic authority, as well as to the wide varieties of Christian groups present in the early centuries of the church, like the mystics (Hylen, 2016).

_____

_____

_____

And, in the following centuries, when martyrdom passed and Christianity moved into the mainstream of life in the Roman world, asceticism took over – the self-inflicted pain of martyrdom up to the point of death.

These women – **the Desert Mothers**, for example – also were known as great mystics.

_____

_____

_____

In the Dark Ages (5th through 8th centuries), there is little record of women mystics but by the **Middle Ages**, around the 9th through 14th centuries, there is more evidence of women mystics with increased themes of love, physical connection, and union with God.

Mechthild of Magdeburg, born around 1210, was one of these. She was well-born, possibly of nobility, and lived in what became Germany. She wrote one book, _The Flowing Light of the Godhead_, which was probably compiled from writings she made over a fifteen-year period about her visions.

> _"I cannot dance, O Lord, unless Thou lead me. If Thou will that I leap joyfully then must Thou Thyself first dance and sing! Then will I leap for love, from love to knowledge, from knowledge to fruition, from fruition to beyond all human sense. There will I remain and circle evermore._

"My body is in long torment, my soul in high delight, for she has seen and embraced her Beloved. Through Him, alas for her! she suffers in torment. As He draws her to Himself, she gives herself to Him... She is engulfed in the glorious Trinity in high union" (Gies, 1978).

Mechthild also described heaven and hell. Heaven includes ten choirs:
"In the first choir is happiness... in the second choir is meek-ness, in the third choir is love, in the fourth sweetness, in the fifth joyfulness, in the sixth noble tranquility, in the seventh riches, in the eighth worthiness, in the ninth burning love, and in the sweet beyond is pure holiness..." (Wilson, 1984).

Hell, instead, is an abyss:
"I have seen a place – its name is Eternal Hatred. It is built in the deepest abyss of the stones of mortal sin. Pride was the first stone... Disobedience, covetousness, gluttony, unchastity were four heavy stones... anger, falseness, and murder – lying betrayal, despair..." (Wilson, 1984).

_____

_____

_____

Hadewijch, writing between 1220 and 1240, was another writer of the Middle Ages.

She wrote in a dialect called Brabant, which means she wrote some-where in the southern Netherlands. She describes visions showing she might have been a nun, but she could have also been a lay woman, or even an artistic recluse.

She wrote poetry that supported a spiritual revival of the time, all written in the style of courtly love songs! (Several examples of that are included in the Definition of Mysticism.)

"The nature from which true love springs has twelve hours which drive love out of herself and bring her back in herself. And when love comes back in herself she brings with her all that makes the unspeakable hours drive her out of herself: a mind that seeks to know, a heart full of desire, a soul full of love. And when love brings these back she throws them into the abyss of the mighty nature in which she was born and nurtured. Then the unspeakable hours enter nature unknown. Then love has come to herself and rejoices in her nature, below, above, and around. And all whose who stay below this knowledge shudder at those who have fallen into the abyss and work there and live and die. For such is love's command and her nature" (Wilson, 1984).

For Hadewijch, in the first unspeakable hour, love reveals its nature to the soul. In the second, the heart tastes death; in the third, love shows *"how one may die and live in her, and how one cannot love without great suffering."*

In the fourth, love makes the soul taste love's hidden designs; in the fifth, love seduces the heart and soul; in the sixth, love despises reason; seventh, *"nothing can dwell in love or touch her except desire"*; and the eighth brings bewilderment.

The ninth hour brings *"love's fiercest storm"*; in the eleventh *"love possesses the beloved by force"*; and in the twelfth, love becomes utterly satisfied in her nature (Wilson, 1984).

_____

_____

_____

Marguerite Porete, also quoted in the Definition of Mysticism document, lived in France, in the late 13th and 14th centuries.

Her work, *Mirror of Simple Souls,* was burned as heretical by a bishop between 1296 and 1306. She herself was condemned as a heretic in 1310 and burned to death.

Marguerite wrote in parts: first, a section where Love speaks or has a dialog with the Soul; and then a second section where Marguerite expounds on what Love has said.

This devise was used in a series of more than 100 articles, several of which describe the seven states of the soul. The soul begins by being touched by God and beholds God and beholds itself affected by the love of God. In the fourth state, the

> *"Soul is drawn up by highness of love through meditation into delight of thought, and abandons all outward labors and obedience to others for highness of contemplation. Then the Soul is so difficult, noble, and delightful that she cannot suffer anything to touch her, except the touch of Love's pure delight which makes her singularly charming and gay, which makes her proud of an abundance of love. Then she is mistress of radiance, that is to say the light of her soul, which causes her to be marvelously filled with love of great faith through the concord of union which put her in possession of her delights"* (Wilson, 1984).

In the fifth state, the soul beholds that God is what all things are and that the Soul is not. In the sixth, the soul sees neither God nor herself, *"But God sees Himself in her through His divine majesty that illuminates this Soul of Himself, so that she sees that no one is but God Himself Who is that of Whom all things are…"*

She describes God's goodness as God's own self so that when the soul is given goodness it has been given God's own self. And the seventh state, *"… keeps Love within the Soul to give us everlasting glory; which we will not know until our soul has left our body"* (Wilson, 1984).

A final woman to mention in this era, is **Julian of Norwich**. She is more well-known than most of the others I've mentioned so far.

Julian lived in England in the 15th century and wrote just one work – *Revelations of Divine Love*. It contained recounts of her sixteen visions (or "showings" as the writing is often called) in the process of her union with God. *Revelations* tries to hold together the love of God for humanity with her era's emphasis on sin and judgment.

> *"And I saw no difference between God and our nature but that it was all God; and yet my understanding discerned that our nature is in God, that is to say, that God is God and our nature is both created and part of God. For the almighty truth of the Trinity is our Father, since He made us and keeps us in Him. And the deep wisdom of the Trinity is our Mother, in whom we are enclosed. And the high goodness of the Trinity is our Lord, and in Him we are enclosed and He in us.*

> *"For at the same time that God united Himself to our body through a maiden's womb, He took our lower nature, and by so doing, He enclosed us all within Himself, uniting Himself to our nature... Thus our Lady is our mother, in whom we shall be enclosed – and Christ was born of her, and she, who is mother of our Savior, is our very mother in whom we will be endlessly borne and whom we shall never leave.*

> *"And this in our Creation God almighty is our kindly Father, and God Who is all wisdom is our kindly Mother, with the love and the goodness of the Holy Ghost – all of Whom are one God and one Lord. And in this joining and uniting, He is our true spouse and we His beloved wife and His fair maiden, with which He was never displeased, for He says: 'I love you and you love Me, and our love shall never part in two'"* (Wilson, 1984).

For reflection…

Did you notice how many of the women mystics talk about the mystic union in terms of a process with steps or stages?

_____

_____

_____

Why do you think that might be?

_____

_____

_____

Is there a connection to modern theories of faith development?

_____

_____

_____

Chapter Five: Renaissance & Enlightenment Christian Women Mystics

Renaissance & Enlightenment Christian Women Mystics

The Renaissance period, in the 15th and 16th centuries, and the Enlightenment era in the 17th-19th centuries, continued to give evidence of Christian women mystics, with varying styles of writing and in a widening geography.

We can read the work of mystic women from Africa, Central America, England, France, Italy, Russia, Spain, South America, the United States, and other areas.

Some of these continue the courtly romantic style of writing but all of them continue the theme of love and its accompanying ecstasy.

I am just going to touch on the wealth of information we have about these women.

Catherine of Bologna (1413-1463, Italy) was an educated woman, who turned her back on typical life and entered a convent, the Poor Clares.

She taught Latin and Tuscan and wrote in both languages. She was an artist and patron of the arts, as well as abbess of her convent.

Her book, *Weapons of the Spirit*, was written in 1438 and was based on her visions. It describes weapons that the younger nuns could use to control their selves and defeat evil.

> *"In the name of the Eternal Father and of His only begotten son, Christ Jesus, the splendor of this paternal glory; in my love for Him I exclaim with a joyful heart and say to His most beloved servants and brides: 'Every lover who loves the Lord come to the dance singing of love. Come dancing and be utterly ablaze. Yearn only for your Creator, who has freed you from the perilous state of the world and has placed you in the most noble cloister of holy religion.*

"I do not want to be parted from that excellent virtue called Hope. Speaking to me, Hope said in her courtesy that I shall truly be able to mount aloft to Heaven, if in this world I have not place to rest my head, that I shall find the greatest pleasure there, if I always have some grief to bear here; that I shall be greatly honored there, if I am despised, afflicted, and troubled here; that I shall be satisfied in Paradise, if I never have what I want here; that I shall sing sweetly in the presence of my God, if I chant psalms humbly in the choir; that he will make me immortal, if here I do not fear death or pain; that I shall be empress of His kingdom if I live here poor and mendicant; and that, if I persevere in His most chaste and virginal love, without doubt I shall rejoice with Him for eternity" (Wilson, 1987).

I've quoted from **Catherine of Genoa** (1447-1510, Italy) in the Definition of Mysticism chapter - the opening paragraph to her *Biography*.

At 16, Catherine was married against her wishes to a dissolute husband who drove her to isolation. On March 20, 1473, she had an experience of being overwhelmed by the enormity of God's love. She converted her husband; after that, they lived together as brother and sister, and began working (and eventually living) at a local hospital.

She focused on the via negative – the "way of negation" - or the understanding that God is incomprehensible so we cannot name God or even speak of God. *"All that can be said about God, is not God."*

With that belief, one must deny all one's ideas or thoughts about God, reduce everything to nothing – but in that process nothing becomes everything! *"My Me is God."*

The human gets lost in, absorbed by, the divine – and, in doing that, becomes itself divine.

_____
_____

_____

My understanding of **Teresa of Avila** (1515-1582, Spain) continues to expand the more I read about her as well as the more I read by her. At first, I had a rather flat view of her: another mystic who wrote about a series of visions she had.

But the story goes deeper. Far from being shut away from life, she traveled extensively, planting convents, and reforming the Carmelite order of nuns. She wrote about her visions but also instructions for nuns and convent life.

But her story is deeper than that, too! A beautiful woman with a strong sense of humor, she enjoyed entertaining and being entertained, even during her early convent life. There was some sort of romance in her early adolescent life and rumors of sexual misconduct when she was older.

Those she brushed off with a laugh saying that they were only fair that since no one had believed the indiscretions of her early life (Flinders, 2009).

But whether she was a saint or a sinner – most likely both! – she shared that common experience of all these women: the mystical experience of union with God.

In chapter 10 of *The Life of Teresa of Avila*, she writes,

"... there would come to me unexpectedly such a feeling of the presence of God as made it impossible for me too doubt that He was within me, or that I was totally engulfed in Him. This was no

kind of vision; I believe it is called Mystical theology. The soul is then so suspended that it seems entirely outside itself. The will loves; the memory is, I think, almost lost, and the mind, I believe, though it is not lost, does not reason – I mean that it does not work, but stands as if amazed at the many things it understands. For God wills it to realize that it understands nothing at all of what His Majesty places before it" (Avila,16th century).

Her self-understanding, her understanding of people, and her understanding of God, go far beyond what others might have expected of her in her youth, but all of it is built on a willingness to give up understanding in the presence of the love of God.

Afro-Peruvian **Ursula de Jesus** *(1604-1666, Peru)* was born into slavery and entered a convent as a teenager. She entered as a slave not a novice, but over time became engaged in the religious life. As her faith grew, her mystical experiences and visions grew as well.

In 1650, she began keeping a journal that told about convent life, but also gave a glimpse into the racial inequities of Christianity at the time.

The Lamp Magazine's website says that Ursula de Jesus "articulates a theology of humility in which nestle the first beginnings of a theology of liberation" (*Lamp*, 2020).

And Valerie Benoist, in *Sister Ursula de Jesus' Equal Economy of Salvation,* writes that Ursula's diary gives a place to argue for "more equal access to the economy of salvation and more solidarity between black catholic women..." (Benoist, 2019).

The Lamp describes a vision from Ursula's diary.

"One of the first visions she describes showed her a black woman who had been enslaved in the convent, María Bran. Ursula sees her in purgatory, dressed in a priest's alb and crowned in flowers, "her face a resplendent black." The woman says that "[s]he was very thankful to God, who with His divine providence had taken her from her land and brought her down such difficult and rugged roads in order to become a Christian and be saved."

"But the Christianity taught to slaves has left Ursula with an urgent, heartbreaking question: "I asked whether black women went to heaven[.]" María Bran says yes, God's mercy will save black women who give Him thanks.

"Later Ursula writes, "Although He raised us as different nations, the will of blacks and whites is the same. In memory, understanding, and will, they are all one. Had He not created them all in His image and likeness and redeemed them with His blood?" (Lamp, 2020).

The translator of her diary - *The Spiritual Diary of a Seventeenth-Century Afro-Peruvian Mystic, Ursula de Jesús* - Nancy van Deusen, writes that one of the nuns in the convent eventually bought Ursula's freedom in 1645.

Her writings bring not only a view of mysticism in her time and place, but also a view of the "complexities of racial inequality," and an exploration of "the power of the written word." (Deusen, 2004)

_____

_____

_____

Ann Lee (1736-1784, United States) was born in Manchester, England, to poor but respectable parents; her mother was very religious, and so was Ann. Even as a child she experienced "divine manifestations" and from her early youth she was strongly against any forms of sexuality, even between married couples (History, 2018).

She was married, unhappily, and bore and lost 4 children in a few short years, bringing about great emotional suffering.

In 1758, she joined a Shaking Quakers society led by James & Jane Wardley – attracted to their strict views on sin and confession. She was arrested for disturbing the peace multiple times – perhaps due to her mental health problems or perhaps because of the unusual worship style of the Shaking Quakers (History, 2018).

Her biography -*Testimonies of the Life, Character, Revelations and Doctrine of Our Ever Blessed Mother Ann Lee, and the Elders with Her, Through whom the Word of Eternal Life was opened in this day of Christ's Second Appearing, Collected from Living Witnesses, in Union with the Church* - recounts one of those imprisonments, in about 1770.

> *(She) "was, at times, filled with visions and revelations of God. By this mean the way of God, and the nature of His work, gradually opened upon her mind, with increasing light and understanding. ...she received a full revelation of the root and foundation of human depravity... she clearly saw whence and wherein all mankind ere lost and separated from God, and the only possible way of recovery" (Testimonies, 1888).*

According to some sources, four years later another revelation told her to establish a Shaker Church in America. Other sources suggest she saw the spiritual awakening there as an escape from the persecution she was facing in England.

In America, her marriage ended but she and her brother began the Shaker Church, founded on mystic spirituality along with social ideas such as: all property being held in common, celibacy, gender and racial equality, intellectual and artistic development, simplicity of dress, and agriculture-based economics.

Over time, she continued to have bouts of severe suffering

interspersed with wonderful visions of God. *Testimonies of the Life* recalls one of those in those years in New York.

> *"Mother... said, 'The Lord, who brought me over the great waters, has redeemed my soul. I hear the angels sing; I see the glory of God as bright as the sun; I see multitudes of the dead, who were slain in battle, arise and come into the first resurrection; I see Christ put crowns on their heads of bright, glorious, and changeable colors. I converse with Christ: I feel Him present with me, as sensibly as I feel my hands together. My soul is married to him in the spirit; he is my husband; it is not I that speaks; it is Christ who dwells in me'"* *(Testimonies, 1888).*

The Women's History Blog points out that despite Ann's convictions about celibate purity and confession of sins, she was a "progressive 18th-century woman."

She was a pioneer for justice "teaching by example the equality of the sexes, economic justice, religious tolerance, and true democracy" (M, 2020).

She also, despite her opposition to lust or sexuality, used language of love and marriage to describe her visions of God and Christ.

_____

_____

_____

In her book, *Religious Experience and Journal of Mrs. Jarena Lee,* giving an account of her call to preach the gospel, **Jarena Lee** (1783-1864, United States) recalls her early life when she was born to a free family in Cape May, NJ and at 7 years of age was sent to live as maid servant.

In her childhood she knew little of religious life but in her early 20's she began to feel a sense of repentance that led her to consider suicide. Over time she felt forgiveness and eventually sanctification by God, which she describes this way:

> *"I retired to a secret place... for prayer, about four o'clock in the afternoon. I had struggled long and hard but found not the desire of my heart. When I rose from my knees.... I again bowed in the same place at the same time, and said "Lord sanctify my soul for Christ's sake." That very instant as if lightening had darted through me, I sprang to my feet, and cried, 'The Lord has sanctified my soul!'*

> *"I ran into the house and told them what happened to me, when, as it were, a new rush of the same ecstasy came upon me, and caused me to feel as if I were in an ocean of light and bliss.... So great was the joy that it is past description"* (Lee, 1849).

Several authors describe her life and writing as a turning point: her sense of self-identity led from an older cultural model for women, particularly women of color, toward a more modern role.

_____

_____

_____

For reflection...

While the Renaissance was a period of growth in literary work, art, music, etc., it was also a time when women's roles were changing to more restricted models. How might that be reflected in these mystic women's faith?

_____

_____

_____

The Enlightenment also brought changes to women's roles in work, education, and society. Again, how might that be reflected here? And how might societal changes be influencing women mystics today?

_____

_____

_____

As we broaden the geography, branches of Christianity, and lifestyles of the women we study, do you find it easier or more difficult to relate to them? Why?

_____

_____

_____

Chapter Six: Early 20th Century Christian Women Mystics

Early 20th Century Christian Women Mystics

I'm skipping over many years and many other women mystics, to move on to one woman who crossed centuries and four other women of the early 20th century: Conceptcion Cabrer de Armida, Lilian Staveley, Edith Stein, Evelyn Underhill, and Simone Weil.

Concepcion Cabrera de Armida (1862-1937, Mexico) – or Conchita as she is known – not only crossed centuries but she also dwelled in that transitional space that several of the Enlightenment era occupied. She represents the variety of lifestyles of mystic women in modernity.

She was a wife and mother of nine children, three of whom died young. Her husband died young as well and she raised her remaining children alone.

Before they had married in 1884, she and her husband had agreed that she could take daily communion and the sacrament played a large role in her mystical experiences. A vision she had after receiving communion - a cross with a pierced beating heart - became the symbol known as the Cross of the Apostolate.

She established multiple religious organizations - like a convent, fraternity, mission, and "crusade" - before her death in 1937. She wrote in her diary that *"To be wife and mother was never a hindrance to my spiritual life."*

She wrote prolifically, leaving behind over 60,000 pages of writings, publishing many books, and providing a model for a mystical life that was fully embedded in the world.

> *"... the Lord opened a door to lavish on me His graces. From that day on how He pursued me! What attention! What tenderness! What astounding kindness toward a miserable creature such as I! He never left me alone neither by day nor by night, neither when I was praying nor when I was not. He kept telling me: 'I want you to be all mine! You are Mine now but I want you to be even more so Mine!' He said over and over:*

'Come. I want to be spiritually married to you. I want to give you My Name and prepare you for great graces'''

"What is happening, Oh my God - I understand - is that this drop of water is lost in the ocean and the nothingness in the infinite. That is, it is not only God who enters into me, even when He penetrates and takes possession of my soul, it is also I who enter into Him. Rather, I am not worthy to enter and I stop at the door, but He takes me in His arms and brings me into these regions unknown to the material world. How rapidly my soul covers these distances! It knows, it sees, it hears, without seeing nor hearing. It finds itself brought together in one point, but in infinite and eternal point, a point of uncreated love. There only it breathes life, is fulfilled and happy, outside of time" (Diary, 1890).

Conchita was venerated in 1999.

_____

_____

_____

Lilian Staveley (1878-1928, England) was born to an affluent family and gives us another view of the mystic lifestyle (Biography, 2018).

Her early life was not one of outward religious observance but the wealthy and privileged world of balls and suitors. She wrote about that time:

> *"I was worshipping the Beautiful without giving sufficient thought to Him from Whom all beauty proceeds. Half a lifetime was to go by before I realized to what this habit was leading me—that it was the first step towards the acquirement of that most exquisite of all blessings—the gift of the Contemplation of God."* (Staveley, 2009)

As a young woman she became an atheist; a painful decision with which she struggled for two years. While in Rome, visiting the temples, she was moved by the beauty of her surroundings and *"...a longing for her Lord so painfully real that the longing could not be denied"* (Staveley, 2009).

In 1899, she married Brigadier General William Cathcart Staveley. At the end of World War I, she began anonymously publishing her spiritual writings. It was only after her death that General Staveley learned that his wife of nearly thirty years had led a hidden spiritual life.

In her theology, Staveley struggled with what she called the "feminine principle" – the role of gender in faith and religion. She saw that the leadership of the church across history had looked down on women and believed that God, as well, found her to be not of the "acceptable sex."

She felt such shame in being female that she came to believe that she couldn't worship God with love but only a form of reverent sadness.

Later, she came to the conclusion that the spiritual journey was the same for men and women but that the soul itself was female: "Clothed in the body of either man or woman, the soul is predominantly feminine—the Feminine Principle beloved of, and returning to, the Eternal Masculine of God" (*Biography*, 2018).

_____

_____

_____

Edith Stein (1891-1942, Germany) was born into an observant Jewish family in what was then Germany but is now Poland, but she became an atheist by her teenage years.

In 1916, Stein received a doctorate of philosophy from the University of Göttingen where she studied and worked with Edmund Husserl and Martin Heidegger. But because she was a woman Husserl did not support her submission for an academic chair after graduation.

Reading the autobiography of the mystic St. Teresa of Ávila caused Stein's conversion from atheism to Catholicism in 1921 and she was baptized on January 1, 1922.

She taught at a Dominican nuns' school from 1923 to 1931. In 1932, she became a lecturer at the Institute for Pedagogy at Münster, but antisemitic legislation passed by the Nazi government forced her to resign the post in 1933.

In a letter to Pope Pius XI, she denounced the Nazi regime and asked the Pope to openly denounce the regime, as well, *"to put a stop to this abuse of Christ's name."*

She was received into the Discalced Carmelite Order as a postulant in 1934. Although she moved from Germany to the Netherlands to avoid Nazi persecution, in 1942 she was arrested and sent to the Auschwitz concentration camp, where she died in the gas chamber. She was canonized by Pope John Paul II in 1998 (*Edith*, 2018).

In her book *Spirituality of the Christian Woman* Stein writes:

> *"I would also like to believe that even the relationship of soul and body is not completely similar in man and woman; with woman, the soul's union with the body is naturally more intimately emphasized. ... Woman's soul is present and lives more intensely in all parts of the body, and it is inwardly affected by that which happens to the body...*

> *"This is closely related to the vocation of motherhood. The task of assimilating in oneself a living being which is evolving and growing, of containing and nourishing it, signifies a definite end in itself. Moreover, the mysterious process of the formation of a new creature in the maternal organism represents such an intimate unity of the physical and spiritual that one is well able to understand that this unity imposes itself on the entire nature of woman. But a certain danger is involved*

here. ... The more intimate the relationship of the soul and body is, just so will the danger of the spiritual decline be greater" (Stein, 1996).

Evelyn Underhill (1875-1941, England) was a poet and novelist, as well as a pacifist and mystic. The Evelyn Underhill Association website contributed much of the following information about Underhill.

As a young child she had mystical experiences and started a lifelong quest to understand their meaning. The author and publisher of over 30 books, she described her early mystical insights as:

> *"...abrupt experiences of the peaceful, undifferentiated plane of reality—like the 'still desert' of the mystic—in which there was no multiplicity nor need of explanation"* (Williams, 1943).

Initially an agnostic, she gradually began to acquire an interest in Neoplatonism and from there became increasingly drawn to Catholicism.

Underhill wrote three highly unconventional though profoundly spiritual novels. Her narratives explored the sacramental intersection of the physical with the spiritual.

She then used that sacramental framework very effectively to illustrate the unfolding of a human drama. In her first novel, *The Grey World*, the hero's mystical journey begins with death, moves through reincarnation, beyond the grey world, and into the choice of a simple life devoted to beauty, reflecting Underhill's own serious perspective as a young woman.

> *"It seems so much easier in these days to live morally than to live beautifully. Lots of us manage to exist for years without*

ever sinning against society, but we sin against loveliness every hour of the day" (Underhill, 1904).

The Lost Word and *The Column of Dust* are also concerned with the problem of living in two worlds and reflect the writer's own spiritual challenges. In the 1909 novel, her hero encounters a rift in the solid stuff of her universe:

> *"She had seen, abruptly, the insecurity of those defenses which protect our illusions and ward off the horrors of truth. She had found a little hole in the wall of appearances; and peeping through, had caught a glimpse of that seething pot of spiritual forces whence, now and then, a bubble rises to the surface of things"* (Underhill, 1909).

For Underhill, mystical experience seems inseparable from an enhancement of consciousness or expansion of perceptual and aesthetic horizons—to see things as they are, in their meanness and insignificance when viewed in opposition to the divine reality, but in their luminosity and grandeur when seen bathed in divine radiance (*Evelyn*, 2019).

Underhill's *Mysticism: A Study of the Nature and Development of Man's Spiritual Consciousness*, was published in 1911. In it she states that (1) mysticism is practical, not theoretical, (2) mysticism is an entirely spiritual activity, (3) the business and method of mysticism is love. (4) mysticism entails a definite psychological experience (Underhill, 1911).

I would add here that one of my favorite mystics, Dorothee Soelle, echoes Underhill's 1st point, when she writes that mystics join with God, see the world through God's eyes, and then returns to the world to live with "eyes wide open" (Soelle, 2001).

_____
_____
_____

After completing her education **Simone Weil** (1909-1943, France) became a professor. She taught intermittently throughout the 1930s, although she took several breaks due to poor health and to devote herself to political activism.

Weil was politically active from early childhood - helping unions to organize and work together collaboratively, involvement with Marxists and Anarchists, fighting in the Spanish Civil War, and spending more than a year working as a laborer so she could better understand the working class.

She sometimes gave away most her income and lived in the most frugal of circumstances.

Unusual among twentieth century intellectuals, she became more religious and inclined towards mysticism as her life progressed. Weil wrote throughout her life, although most of her writings did not attract much attention until after her death.

Weil's mysticism included a focus on absence: God is utter fullness thus creation exists where God is not. However, that was offset by a concept from Plato's philosophy: metaxy, the idea that the wall between prisoners separates them but by rapping on that wall, they can communicate.

In Weil's words:
"Every separation is a link" (Weil, 1947).

Her mysticism also included a common understanding among mystics: that affliction is a part of the spiritual life, it goes beyond mental and physical suffering to spiritual suffering. Like absence, affliction is also offset by a focus on beauty.

> *"The beautiful is the experimental proof that the incarnation is possible... Beauty captivates the flesh in order to obtain permission to pass right through the soul."* (Weil, 1947).

Weil's whole life was marked by an exceptional compassion for the suffering of others; at the age of five, she refused to eat sugar after she heard that soldiers fighting WWI had to go without.

She died at 34, from malnutrition during WWII after refusing to eat more than the minimal rations she believed were available to soldiers at the time.

In *Gravity and Grace, she wrote:*
> *"God's love for us is not the reason for which we should love him. God's love for us is the reason for us to love ourselves. ... If we want a love which will protect the soul from wounds we must love something other than God"* (Weil, 1947).

And in a letter, she wrote:

> *"I hereby include the English poem that I recited to you, Love [by George Herbert]; it played a big role in my life, for I was busy reciting it to myself at the moment when, for the first time, Christ came to take me. I believed I was merely resaying a beautiful poem, and unbeknownst to myself, it was a prayer.* (*Simone*, 2018)

_____
_____
_____

For reflection…

Did the lives of these 20th Century women seem more familiar than the ancient women mystics?

_____
_____
_____

What similarities might you have found in these women's lives that connect with contemporary life?

_____
_____
_____

What parts of their lives were equally unfamiliar?

_____
_____
_____

What do you find meaningful, helpful, interesting, or challenging about these women and their writing?

_____
_____
_____

Chapter Seven: What Do Women Mystics Say to Us

What Do Women Mystics Say to Us

Part 1: Common Patterns Among Mystics

There seem to be several common patterns among women mystics.

The first is education and writing. In part, this is to be expected. In earlier centuries uneducated women didn't write and so we are less likely to have left behind evidence of their faith.

But it seems that even those who claimed to be uneducated in medieval times were able to read and write. And the 20th century mystics are certainly well educated.

Second, for those 20th century women, there's a pattern of atheism or agnosticism that precedes the mysticism. It would be hard to discern that in the earlier mystics since the idea of not participating in religion was uncommon.

Third, there's a pattern of rejection of typical woman's roles – either on the part of the earlier mystics who rejected money, marriage, and family for faith or the later mystics who were pacifists, activists, liberationists, etc.

And fourth, there's a pattern of illness and suffering in their lives, even among the 20th Century women.

Staveley had an illness of several years duration that prevented her from marrying, Stein died in a Nazi gas chamber, and Weil died of malnutrition after living a brief life of exceptional voluntary poverty.

Some participants in my workshops have also pointed out other themes: beauty and dance and visions and joy, just to name a few!

Some of these themes seem to fit together well: education and the rejection of typical women's roles make some sense. Education and a move away from faith can also make some sense.

But other patterns do not rest easy together and I encourage you to reflect upon them before reading on.

For reflection....

Why would an educated intelligent woman focus on and find redemption in illness and suffering?

_____

_____

_____

Why would an educated and intelligent woman move so quickly from rejecting God to seeking a mystical union with God?

_____

_____

_____

Why would any woman want to connect suffering to that mystical union? Where does love and joy and beauty fit into suffering?

_____

_____

_____

I don't have answers to those questions, but I think we need to recognize the patterns if we are going to discuss whether these women have something to say to us today.

Part II: Transitional Times

Just as I think we must look at patterns in the women mystic's lives, I think we need to look for similarities between their worlds and ours.

Every generation is in a time of change and flux but many of these women were living in great times of transition.

From the mystics and martyrs of the early years of the Christian church to the Middle Ages as Europe moved out of the Dark Ages to the Renaissance to the Enlightenment to World Wars I & II – many of these mystics were living in upheaval and change (Petroff, 1992).

So are we. The amount of change that occurred between our grand-parent's time and ours is less than the change we've encountered within a few decades, or sometimes a few years.

Think of how long it took to move from the first telephone to the first cell phone – and how short a time it took to move from that to the smart phones of today.

The first telephone call went out in 1870, the first cell phone call more than 100 years later (1973). The cell phone was the size of a brick, weighed 2.5 pounds, and did nothing but make and receive phone calls.

It took 100 years to untether the phone and less than 50 to bring it down to less than the size of a deck of cards, a weight of only ounces, and the ability to talk to us, guide our travels, and search the internet for our friends, a good restaurant, or a sale.

Transitional times are times of instability, often accompanied by fear, anger, and repression, but also allowing for new ideas and behaviors to develop. A change is made, nothing ever goes back fully to what it once was – for good or bad – and opportunities arise.

Like the discussion of patterns, this is an area without answers, but I invite you to ponder these questions.

For reflection…

Is there any connection between the frequency of women mystics and eras of change?

_____
_____
_____

Is the physical suffering of changing times connected to the mystical experiences of their souls?

_____
_____
_____

Is there any connection between the contemporary interest in mysticism and the transitional nature of our era?

_____
_____
_____

What does all this have to do with love and union with God?

_____
_____
_____

Part III: Gender Differentiation

Another thought about mysticism that might be worth pursuing is gender differences.

There are three ways of looking at differences between men and women.
Men (or women) are innately superior to women (or men).
Men and women are innately different, but both are equally important.
Men and women are innately equal, and any inequalities are caused by nurture, not nature.

When we look at mystic experience, gender often makes an appearance!

This description of the *Comparative Study of Mysticism* (*Mysticism, 2018*) refers to "…neuroscience, where researchers explore electro-chemical brain states associated with mystical experience, in proposing evidence of a mystical neurological substrate."

This, for some less reputable sources I've read in the past, has even suggested that male and female brains process information differently and female brains are more receptive to mystic experiences!

That same study of mysticism, from Stanford University (*Mysticism, 2018*), also points to the gender differences by looking at men's definitions of mysticism as a solitary experience as opposed to women's concerns with the socio-political ramifications of the experience.

That article points out that men tend to see God more as transcendent while women tend to see God as more imminent. It also points out that this is such a new study of mysticism that we don't know where it will lead.
Similarly, Grace M. Jantzen's book *Power, Gender and Christian Mysticism*, discusses the relationship of mysticism and power in medieval times (Jantzen, 1996).

A third area in this topic was discussed in the Journal for the Scientific Study of Religion (Society, 2020) which has done various studies on mysticism, one of which implied a connection between mysticism and unexpected stress.

While I have not read that work, perhaps their investigation might give some insight into the stress of women's lives (in the past and today) that might affect their mystic experiences.

Again, I have more questions than answers, so I encourage you to simply reflect on these questions.

For reflection:

It makes sense to me that stress and suffering go hand in hand. But how does that relate to love?

_____
_____
_____

And what role does power and the search for power play in all of this?

_____
_____
_____

If women have a different view of God from men, a different approach to mystic experience, and a different socio-political perspective – how might that play out in church life as women become the majority players in church life?

_____
_____
_____

Chapter 8: Conclusion

Conclusion

All of which brings me back to the question I posed in the introduction of this book: do these women have anything of value to say to us today?

Do their situations, their experiences, their writings – in whole or in part – tell us something that we can apply to our faith today?

Can they shed light on our desire for God, our desire for faithfulness, our desire for unity, our desire for understanding?

Can they tell us anything that makes sense of the dance we have been in throughout our lives – or the dancing yet to come?

I recommend a deconstructive conversation as you end these readings. Find a thread and pull it till something unravels and an ah-ha moment happens!

Look for anything here that reminds you of something you've read from one of the women mystics and see how it might fit together.

There are no right or wrong answers - just be comfortable going where the Spirit leads!

For reflection…

As we look back over the women we've read about and discussed, do they have anything to say to us today? Do they have anything to tell us about our faith?

_____

_____

_____

Do their experiences, situations, writings, etc. tell us anything we could apply to our faith? Can they shed light on our desire for God, our desire for unity, our desire for understanding?

_____

_____

_____

And where are you going next with this? Are there women you want to read more about?

_____

_____

_____

How might you share the thoughts, teachings, ideas, poetry, music, etc. of these women with others in your congregation or community?

_____

_____

_____

Bibliography

Ayo, N. *The Mysticism of the Golden Rule*

Benoist, V. (Fall 2019). *"Sister Ursula de Jesus' Equal Economy of Salvation"* Publication of the Afro-Latin/American Research Association. Issue 23. oid:10.32855/palara.2019.008

Biography of Lilian Stavely, a contemporary, and secret, Christian mystic. (2018). World Wisdom. http://www.worldwisdom.com/public/authors/Lilian-Staveley.aspx

Cohick, L. H. (2009). *Women in the world of the earliest Christians: illuminating ancient ways of life*. Baker Academic.

Corrigan, J., Denny, F., Jaffee, M. S., & Eire, C. (2011). *Jews, Christians, Muslims: A Comparative Introduction to Monotheistic Religions* (2nd ed.). Routledge.

Deusen, V. N. E. (2004). *The Souls of Purgatory: The Spiritual Diary of a Seventeenth-Century Afro-Peruvian Mystic, Ursula de Jesus (Diálogos Series)* (Illustrated ed.). University of New Mexico Press.

Edith Stein | EWTN. (2018). EWTN Global Catholic Television Network. https://www.ewtn.com/catholicism/library/edith-stein-10180

Eliach, Y. (2011). *Hasidic Tales of the Holocaust*. Van Haren Publishing.

Evelyn Underhill. (2016, August 19). The Evelyn Underhill Association. http://evelynunderhill.org/about/

Fisher, M. P., & Rinehart, R. (2016). *Living Religions (10th Edition) (10th ed.)*. Pearson.

Flinders, C. L. (2009). *Enduring Grace: Living Portraits of Seven Women Mystics.* HarperOne.

Gies, J., & Gies, F. (1978). *Women in the Middle Ages (Medieval Life).* Harper Perennial.

Hirshfield, J. (1995). *Women in Praise of the Sacred: 43 Centuries of Spiritual Poetry by Women (1st ed.).* Harper Perennial.

Hexham, I. (1993). *Concise Dictionary of Religion.* Intervarsity Press.

History of the Shakers (U.S. National Park Service). (2018). National Parks Service. https://www.nps.gov/articles/history-of-the-shakers.htm

Hylen, S. E. (2015). *The Acts of Paul and Thecla.* Oxford

Jantzen, G. M. (1996). *Power, Gender & Christian Mysticism (Cambridge Studies in Ideology and Religion)* (First Paperback ed.). Cambridge University Press.

Julian of Norwich. *Revelations of Divine Love.*

King, U. (2004). *Christian Mystics.* Routledge.

Lee, J. (1849). *Religious Experience and Journal of Mrs. Jarena Lee, Giving an Account of Her Call to Preach the Gospel.* Pub. for the author.

M. (2020, May 24). *Ann Lee.* History of American Women. https://www.womenhistoryblog.com/2008/12/ann-lee.html

Mechthild of Magdeburg. *The Flowing Light of the Godhead*

Mysticism (Stanford Encyclopedia of Philosophy). (2018, July 31). Plato. https://plato.stanford.edu/entries/mysticism/#MystReliExpeGend

Petroff, E. A. (1994). *Body and Soul: Essays on Medieval Women and Mysticism* (1st ed.). Oxford University Press.

Conchita: A Mother's Spiritual Diary by Marie-Michel Philipon (1978–07-05). (1878). Alba House.

Petroff, E. A. (1986) Christian History, Vol. 30. "Medieval Women's Visionary Literature." Oxford.

Porete, Marguerite. Mirror of Simple Souls

R. F. V., Ms.D. (1978). *The Mystic Power of the Golden Rule.* (1st ed.). Fellowship of the Golden Rule.

Richardson, J. L. (2010). *In the Sanctuary of Women: A Companion for Reflection and Prayer* (42495th ed.). Upper Room Books.

Rolf, V. M. (2014). *Julian's Gospel: Illuminating the Life and Revelations of Julian of Norwich* (Reprint ed.). Orbis Books.

Salisbury, J. E. (1997). *Perpetua's Passion*. Routledge.

Sharma, A. (1987). *Women in World Religions.* State University of NY Press.

Society for the Scientific Study of Religion. (2021, December 26). Society for the Scientific Study of Religion. https://sssreligion.org/

Soelle, D., Rumscheidt, B., & Rumscheidt, M. (2001). *The Silent Cry: Mysticism and Resistance*. Fortress Press.

Song, S. J. (August 16, 2018). *John Wesley and Mysticism.* Methodist Theological University Seoul.

Simone Weil (Stanford Encyclopedia of Philosophy). (2018, March 10). Plato. https://plato.stanford.edu/entries/simone-weil/

Stavely, L. Fitzgerald, J. A., & Zaleski, P. (2009). *A Christian Woman's Secret: A Modern-Day Journey to God (Spiritual Classics)* (Illustrated ed.). World Wisdom.

Stein, E. (1996). *The Collected Works of Edith Stein, Volume Two, Edition Two.* ICS Publications.

Swidler, L. (1976). *Women in Judaism: the Status of Women in Formative Judaism.* Scarecrow Press Inc.

Teresa of Avila. *The Life of Teresa of Avila*

Testimonies of the Life, Character, Revelations and Doctrine of Our Ever Blessed Mother Ann Lee, and the Elders with Her, Through whom the Word of Eternal Life was opened in this day of Christ's Second Appearing, Collected from Living Witnesses, in Union with the Church. Second Edition. (1888). Week, Parsons & Co., Printers.

Underhill, E. (1904). *The Grey World.*

Underhill, E. (1907). *The Lost World.*

Underhill, E. (1908). *The Column of Dust.*

Underhill, E. (1911). *Mysticism: A Study of the Nature and Development of Man's Spiritual Consciousness.*

Ursula de Jesus and the fortress of patience. (2020, June 20).

The Lamp Magazine. https://thelampmaga-zine.com/2020/06/18/ursula-de-jesus-and-the-fortress-of-patience/

Wattles, J. (1987). *Levels of Meaning in the Golden Rule.*

Weil, S. (1947). *Gravity and Grace.* Librairie Plon.

Williams, C., editor. (1943). *The Letters of Evelyn Underhill.* Longmans Green.

Wilson, K. M. editor. (1984). *Medieval Women Writers,* University of Georgia Press

Wilson, K. M. (1987). *Women Writers of the Renaissance and Reformation* (First Printing ed.). University of Georgia Press.

Made in the USA
Columbia, SC
18 January 2024